soul survivor

Pressing through the
process of life crises

Carolyn Wagner

Copyright © 2023 by Carolyn Wagner

Soul Survivor
by Carolyn Wagner

Printed in the United States of America

ISBN: 9798858710813

All rights reserved. No part of this document may be reproduced or transmitted in any form, by any means (electronic, photocopying, recording, or otherwise) without the written permission of the author.

Unless otherwise indicated, Bible quotations are taken from the New King James Version®. Copyright © 1982 by Thomas Nelson. Used by permission. All rights reserved.

Scriptures marked (AMPC) are from the Amplified Bible, Classic Edition. Copyright © 1954, 1958, 1962, 1964, 1965, 1987 by The Lockman Foundation.

Contents

Introduction v
Part 1: The Event 1
Part 2: The Journey 7
    The Journey: Day-to-Day Survival 10
    The Journey: Believing God for
    Miracles 13
    The Journey: A Deeper Level of Low 18
    The Journey: Moving On Up 20
Part 3: The Pressing 23
    The Pressing: Purpose 26
    The Pressing: Pain 26
    The Pressing: Pressure 28
    The Pressing: Power 29
    The Pressing: Protection and Provision ... 30
    The Pressing: Problems and Pitfalls 31
Part 4: Conclusion 33
Thirty-One Days of Power 35

Introduction

I'VE JUST BEGUN a new season in my life. It seemed like it took an eternity to arrive, but now that it's upon me, I am having a difficult time even believing that it is here. My eighteen-year single-parent journey came to a screeching halt when the two younger Wagner children became adults. Since that time I have endured much tribulation, but I am living proof of God's faithfulness. It's like the old song says, "Through it all, I've learned to trust in Jesus; I've learned to trust in God." Through it all, I've learned to depend upon His Word.

I am writing this book with the hope it will encourage others in and through their own difficult journeys. I can say like the psalmist said, "It has been good for me to have been afflicted." I have found my purpose in the pain, and my testimony has come by the way of testing. I am wiser, better, and stronger. I've got God's anointing and His favor. I'm still standing, and at the same time, moving forward. "I can do all things through Christ who strengthens me," and, "if God be for me, who can be against me." I have overcome by the "blood of the Lamb, and by the word of my testimony."

And at the risk of sounding a bit cliché, let me add that the struggle produced strength. I am not a victim, but victorious, and I was able to triumph in spite of tragedy. So please know that God is not a respecter of persons, and He will surely do for you what He has done for me. So don't give up now. Keep on pressing forward one second at a time.

You can make it for one more minute and one more hour. It's not an option for you to lay down and die. Know this: God loves you, and He is working on your behalf. He is indeed working all things together for your good and for His eternal purposes. He will take your mess and turn it into a powerful message.

Introduction

As you read on, I can earnestly say to you: "For I consider that the sufferings of this present time are not worthy to be compared with the glory which shall be revealed to us" (Romans 8:18). Nothing can separate you from the love of Jesus Christ, and, "Yet in all these things we are more than conquerors through Him who loved us" (Romans 8:37).

Part 1: The Event

IT WAS APRIL 11, 1994. Four days earlier I had given birth to my fourth child, a baby girl who was also welcomed by her father and three older brothers, aged sixteen months, twelve, and thirteen. I was extremely tired, and the weather outside was ominous that evening. We were experiencing torrential rains in our city, and there was flash flooding. The weather conditions made the arrival of an unfamiliar orange truck all the more disturbing.

When my oldest son shouted out, "There's a man in an orange truck in the driveway," my husband bolted out of the front door faster than the lightening that was flashing in the sky. There I was, alone in the house with a newborn, a toddler, and two middle school-aged boys. As the time dragged on, the children got hungry, and I found myself on edge as I tried to cook some dinner and manage all the commotion. After all, I had just gotten home from the hospital two days prior, and I was in no condition to be doing so much so soon.

As the spaghetti cooked and the children clamored, I grew more and more uneasy. Something just wasn't right. Who was the stranger in the orange truck? Was my husband in some type of trouble? It seemed like an eternity as I waited for my husband to return to the house. I even sent my oldest son outside with an umbrella to coax his father back into the safety of home; however, these efforts were of no avail. Finally, after the three boys and I had already finished dinner, he came back into the house.

He rushed up the stairs, and I followed him in hot pursuit with our new baby girl in my arms. I confronted him. "What's going on? Are you in some kind of trouble? Oh no—it's not some type of financial problem again, is it?" Hundreds of frantic thoughts raced through my mind.

Part 1: The Event

Sure, we had faced some problems before, but something was eerily different now. And then, it happened. The unthinkable, unexpected, and horrific thing happened. "Who is that man in the orange truck?" I demanded. And then, he looked at me with the coldness of a coffin, and said, "I'm having an affair with his wife."

I felt the blood drain from my face. My hands became cold, and my heart pounded in my chest. It felt as if I had been kicked in the stomach, and I felt faint. All I could utter was, *"What?"* I felt confused. I didn't know what to say next. So, I shouted, *"What?* Are you leaving me? What did you say?" I don't remember much of the conversation that followed. I called a friend. I called my mother. I didn't want the older children to hear this conversation. Time stood still, and I felt lost and helpless, unable to cope with the situation at hand.

The days that followed were difficult. I did a lot of yelling and crying. How could this happen? How could the person I had been married to since

I was nineteen years old do something so terrible? What had happened? I struggled to manage my emotions and to care for the children at the same time. I had never felt a pain so intense. I hurt from the inside out. I was angry, angry, angry, and there were many sleepless nights.

Finally, after three excruciating months, my husband moved out of the house to go live with the "other woman." Life became terrifying as I had never walked a rocky path like this one before. Everything changed. I had to take care of numerous practical matters. My children and I were hurting, and I was so overwhelmed with having to care for everyone and everything with no time at all to pull myself together.

What would I do to pay the bills and put food on the table? I had taken an extended maternity leave after the birth of our fourth child, and my husband was gone. I had gone from a dual-income household to a zero-income household. There really are not words in our human language to describe the depth of pain, confusion, and

Part 1: The Event

anguish that I felt. Yet in spite of all of the turmoil, I did know that the only one who could truly help me was Jesus. And all I could do was to fall into His arms.

Part 2: The Journey

I'M CERTAIN YOU'VE heard the expression, "Life is hard, but God is good." Sometimes we just don't know how good God really is until life is hard. And my life had gotten hard—really hard. Life hadn't been hard up until this time. No one but God could have prepared me for this trial, and no one but God could have given me the strength and the grace to endure this trial.

Enduring hardship as a good soldier of Jesus Christ became my challenge. Over the days, months, weeks, and years, my children and I were faced with numerous obstacles. How can life go on after tragedy?

Eventually, my family, church family, and friends became aware of my situation. People wanted to help but didn't know how to help. Some people didn't know what to say, so they didn't say anything. Some people said hurtful things like, "If you'd been a better wife, your husband wouldn't have left you," or, "I saw your husband at the mall with his girlfriend." I had to learn to forgive people for not understanding. I had to forgive people for adding to my pain. I had to do a lot of forgiving so I could stay focused on the task of living.

I did my best to take care of practical matters. I qualified for emergency food stamps and medical assistance. That was God's way of making certain I could feed my family. I was too broken to really care how God provided; I was just grateful that He did. Humility was the key. I had to accept whatever blessing God sent my way, however He chose to send it.

I tried so hard to meet the needs of my children, but the task was at best overwhelming. I desperately needed healing for myself, yet in spite of my own sufferings, I wasn't the only one suffering. As one could imagine, my older children were not coping well with the departure of their father.

Part 2: The Journey

I was physically, mentally, and emotionally exhausted. With little or no strength to meet each day, all I could do was to pray and ask the Lord to help me. Caring for two teenagers and two babies all by myself took everything I had, and then some. I soon came to learn that God's power was made perfect in my weakness. True enough I was weak mentally, physically, and emotionally; however, I was spiritually strong.

Prior to the event, the Lord had been moving so mightily in my life. I had experienced a spiritual growth explosion. Only a few years prior had I recommitted to living my life totally and completely for Jesus. I was baptized in the name of Jesus, and just months later God filled me with His precious Holy Spirit.

As I learned to pray in my new heavenly language, I grew stronger and stronger in my faith. I had a renewed hunger and thirst for the things of God, and I pursued Him with a passion. Little did I know that this was truly the time of preparation for the testing that was about to come.

Each day I had to trust God for the strength to live and make it through the next twenty-four hours. My days were filled with emotional pain, suffering, struggles, strife, and much hard work. All of this was too much for me to handle, and I let the Lord know that it was never in my book of plans to be a single parent. He let me know that His grace was sufficient.

All I could really do was cling to the Lord and survive. I just had to make it one day at a time. Little did I know that God had big plans for this trial. He was there, ready, willing, and able to display His awesome power in my life, and in the lives of my children.

The Journey: Day-to-Day Survival

Nothing was the same. Life as I had known it had ended. Each and every day presented some type of new challenge. My body was still healing from childbirth, and there seemed to be no way possible to even think about emotional healing.

Part 2: The Journey

Just as there are varying degrees of wounds in our bodies, so are there varying degrees of wounds in our emotional being and spirit. It seemed as if a nuclear bomb had been dropped right in the center of my family. I now had to trust the Lord on a whole new level. After all, I was alone with four children and only a very few dollars in the bank. God was so faithful.

Members from my church family provided meals for us. Other precious saints brought diapers, and the Lord knew that was a definite need with not one, but two children in diapers at the time. Slowly but steadily, the Lord sent financial assistance through family and many unexpected sources.

God was teaching me that He would supply all of my needs. Sure, I had always believed that He had and would supply my needs; however, with no certain finances coming into the house, I had to trust Him so much more.

The summer months were very challenging with the two older children now on summer break from school. They had to take on a paper route to bring some income into the house. I knew that eventually I would need to return to work as a teacher; however, I did not want to work full time with a new baby, three other children, and family trauma.

It is difficult to put into words how much emotional pain there was in my home. We prayed, read the Bible, and went to church three times per week. I wasn't getting much rest due to the baby having her nights and days reversed for quite some time. Physically there was also pain. I had never quite recovered from a severe pain in my left lower back that ran down the entire length of my left leg, and eventually I had to have major back surgery to repair a ruptured disc.

All I could do was to trust the Lord for a few minutes at a time. There were so many pressures with children, finances, health, exhaustion, uncertainty, etc. I didn't have time to develop a plan or strategy for dealing with this crisis. Trusting Jesus was my only plan.

Part 2: The Journey

The Journey: Believing God for Miracles

Each day was a microtrial. It was difficult at best to try to find some type of routine or normalcy. I didn't want my marriage to end. I wanted my family to be reunited, healed, and restored. I prayed every day for God to intervene. I had never hurt this much before, emotionally or physically. The Lord continued to provide all of our needs. It was amazing to see the hand of God moving so powerfully in the midst of tragedy.

I can specifically recall one night after the children had gone to sleep, I went downstairs and sat on the sofa, wondering how I could possibly make it through all of these problems. All of a sudden, I could sense such a strong presence of the Lord. There is really no way to describe His presence other than it is an overwhelming feeling of love and peace.

I opened my Bible to Isaiah 43 and began reading. It was as if Jesus was sitting right beside me as He said these words: "But now, thus says the LORD, who created you, O *Carolyn,* and He who formed you, O *Carolyn*: 'Fear not, for I have redeemed you; I have called you by your name. You are mine. When you pass through the waters, I will be with you; and through the rivers, they shall not overflow you. When you walk through the fire, you shall not be burned, Nor shall the flame scorch you. For I am the LORD your God, The Holy One of Israel, your Savior.' " He said, "Fear not for I am with you" (Isaiah 43:1-3; 5).

Over the days, weeks, months, and years, this word from the Lord brought me much comfort and strength. Words have such power. Early on in my trial, my pastor, Jack Greenwood, told me that even though this trial had come when I was very weak physically, spiritually I was very strong. His encouragement also gave me further impetus to keep moving forward in the face of adversity. God's hand was on my life and on the lives of my children.

August arrived, and school began for the two oldest children. They were both in middle school;

Part 2: The Journey

one in seventh grade and one in eighth grade. Miracle provision from the Lord continued, but I knew I needed to work. I prayed the Lord would bless me with something part time to begin. It would be too much stress to try to work full time with the weight of the family crisis and two babies at home; one just four months old now and the other twenty months old.

Again, God was faithful. It was open house at the middle school where the older boys attended, and it just so happened that several years earlier I had been a math teacher at this school. As we were about to leave the school for the evening, Mr. Jones, the principal, greeted me in the hallway. He was the assistant principal during the years I had taught there previously. All of a sudden and very unexpectedly, Mr. Jones asked me if I would be interested in teaching part time for him!

God is nothing short of amazing. Mr. Jones said I would teach two sections of math and monitor one study hall. And to make matters even better, the school was only two miles from our house. I will always remember that night. Of course, I told Mr. Jones I would be honored to apply for the position.

I applied, and I got the job. All glory be to God! Now all I needed was childcare. God provided again as a dear friend came to my home each day with her baby and took care of my babies as well, and I would only be gone from the house for about two-and-a-half hours each day. God is good!

Shortly after I began teaching, the pain in my back traveling down through my left leg intensified. It worsened to the point that I was no longer able to sleep, and there was no relief from the pain either standing, sitting, or lying down.

After a trip to the doctor and some diagnostic testing, I learned I would need to have surgery to repair a ruptured disc in my spine. Apparently the disc had ruptured during the birth of my fourth child, my daughter. How could this be? Another tragedy within a tragedy. How could I possibly

Part 2: The Journey

have surgery? Who would take care of the children, and what about my new job?

Of course, the Lord was faithful through it all. He provided precious people to come to my house and help out. The surgery went well, and due to much prayer, I was able to recover in two weeks as opposed to the expected six weeks. I had been in so much pain that the surgery was an actual relief. I struggled to walk, but miraculously I was able to get back on my feet in not much time at all.

I can recall so many nights before bedtime holding my baby tightly in my arms and rocking while I cried and sang, "Oh how He loves you and me. Oh, how He loves you and me. He gave His life, what more could He give? Oh, how He loves me. Oh, how He loves you. Oh, how He loves you and me."

I had to remind myself how much God did love me and my children because when times get so tough, it's easy for the enemy to tell you, "If God loved you, you wouldn't be going through all of this suffering." That is a lie from the pit of hell. What the enemy means for harm in our lives, God turns it around for our good and for His glory!

The Journey: A Deeper Level of Low

As time went by, each day seemed like an eternity. With four children to care for, bills to pay, work, and everything else, I was in way over my head. I was praying for my marriage to be restored and believed that God was big enough to do that. It seemed like every day came with some type of crisis within the major crisis. I rarely got any sleep simply due to the nature of single parenting. With teenagers and babies in the house there wasn't much time for rest.

I was literally drowning in a sea of stress. I prayed and cried, and sometimes I cried more than I prayed. I had way too many responsibilities to keep up with and there wasn't much physical help from anyone. Other people had their own lives to manage. It was during this time that

Part 2: The Journey

I truly came to understand that *all* of my help comes from the Lord. I truly believe that we learn He is all we need when He is all we've got.

I did the best I could do. I trusted the Lord to supply what I needed. He did send people into our lives to help us out from time to time, and I was so thankful! I just wanted out of this painful predicament. I didn't want to be a single parent and I wanted God to fix everything.

My faith in God was strong until one day there was an unexpected knock at the door. When I opened the door, a man handed me some papers and explained that I would need to appear in court for divorce proceedings.

I froze with unbelief. I couldn't believe what I was hearing. After two-and-a-half years of waiting, suffering, and praying for a miracle, things were going to end with a divorce? All of my hopes and dreams were shattered, and I sunk to a new level of low. Depression set in and I felt hopeless.

The Journey: Moving On Up

My mother told me the divorce was going to hurt more than I was anticipating. It was very difficult for me to wrap my mind around this concept because I was already in so much pain. My mother was correct. On January 2, 1997, the gavel hit the judge's podium and declared the final dissolution of our marriage.

Yes indeed, my mother was correct. At this point in time, I was so far down that all I could do was to move up. When I returned home, I stared aimlessly out of the large front picture window. My picture of life had been shattered once again.

How could I move forward and get out of this pit? What next? It was wintertime both in the natural world and in my life. In the dead of winter everything looks cold and bleak. The harsh coldness of the wind and barrenness of the trees only reinforced how I was feeling on the inside.

I had believed God for a miracle, and it hadn't happened. Little did I know that the true miracle

Part 2: The Journey

that would happen was going to happen in me! In the years that followed, life continued to be nearly unmanageable. There were so many obstacles—too many to enumerate.

I was hurting and so were my children. Holidays were especially horrible. It seemed as if everything reminded me of what I had lost. Eventually I had to learn to focus on what I *had*, and not what I had lost. Our home was filled with love, pain, anger, and suffering, yet we had to move forward the best that we could.

I fought depression for several years while at the same time having to literally force myself to continue to care for my children and every other responsibility that is imaginable. I remember hoping I could just check into the psychiatric ward of the hospital just to escape all of the pressure. I'm certainly glad God didn't grant that desire, but instead He continued to give me grace and strength.

Years went by until one day I woke up and literally declared, "God—I am tired of just surviving; You have got to move me into living once again." And He did. He taught me how to press through the process!

Part 3: The Pressing

GOD IS A God of processes. He is also a God of order and precision, and He knows exactly what to do and when to do it. *Process* can be defined as a series of actions, changes, or functions that achieve an end or specified result. A process is also a passage of time. Little did I know it, but all along I was moving through a process in God's school. He was preparing me to fulfill His calling on my life, and at the time I had no idea! I had to keep on pressing through the process.

As I continued to grow and mature in the Lord, I understood that God's processes require waiting. I did *not* want to be a single parent, but I found myself having to submit to this season with no promise of it ending any time soon.

God is the one who predetermines the length of all of life's processes, and in order for us to continue to keep moving forward and advancing in the purposes of God we must be willing to submit to *His* timing.

However, we can often become disappointed and disillusioned because of our own wrong expectations in terms of our timing versus God's timing. But God is precise. He is clear, exact, distinct, and purposeful; therefore, we can trust Him to safely navigate us through all of our processes.

It is our responsibility to follow His lead and *press* through each process. Keep doing the next right thing. Keep trusting; keep praying; keep reading the Bible; keep on keeping on! Keep on pressing.

Pressing means that we keep moving forward. It is a constant progression. Pressing necessitates that we keep advancing in the face of adversity. Pressing is a posture that declares I am determined to not look back, quit, or give up. It continues to exert steady force against the kingdom of darkness, and pressing forward results in a favorable outcome as God's favor surrounds our lives.

Part 3: The Pressing

Another definition of the word *press* is to clasp or embrace closely. Inasmuch as we press against the kingdom of darkness, we must press into Jesus as we embrace His Word and cling to His promises. And on another note, it is important to remember that as we continue to press, we are going to *be pressed.* In other words, we are going to continue to be placed in constraining circumstances for the strengthening of our faith and to the glory of God.

Just like olives must be pressed and crushed in order for the oil to be extracted, our submission to the times of pressing and crushing will result in the increase of God's anointing on our lives. It is so important to have a willing heart that allows the Lord to lead us through these processes. My greatest trial became my greatest ministry—I pressed through the process.

The Pressing: Purpose

First and foremost, there is a purpose for our process. God does not waste our pain, mistakes, bad choices, or suffering. God has a unique plan for each person He creates, and it is never a surprise to God what happens in our lives.

In John 16:33, Jesus tells us we are going to have trials, tribulations, and issues in our lives, but we can be cheerful in knowing that He has overcome all of these things. God takes the things that were meant to harm us and turns them around for our good. Romans 8:28 declares that all of these things are working together for our good, and fitting into God's overall plan for our lives.

The Pressing: Pain

It is paramount for us to understand that there will be pain and suffering as we press through the process. Understanding this concept will help us to let go of the unrealistic expectation that we will

Part 3: The Pressing

not hurt. We were never promised that we would be exempt from pain. There is pain in the process.

Letting go can be painful. Grieving is painful. Emotional wounds run deep, and they take time to heal. But as we learn to embrace this pain and allow it to draw us nearer to Jesus, we will move forward into the promises and blessings of God.

When I learned that my husband had been unfaithful and was leaving our family, the pain in my soul was excruciating—nothing like I had ever felt before. I prayed and told the Lord I never wanted to feel a pain of that magnitude again. It took me years to heal, but by the grace of God I did heal.

You see, if I had never felt this pain, I would have never known that Jesus could, in fact, heal this pain. I knew Him to be a physical healer but didn't know that He could also heal my mind and emotions.

I am healed and whole, set free by the blood of Jesus. Because of His suffering on earth and on the cross, He could understand my pain and provide the healing I needed. I had to keep on pressing for this blessing, but the joy that was set before me was worth it.

The Pressing: Pressure

Along with all the pain came much pressure. Diamonds begin as carbon. They are formed through immense amounts of pressure and heat. If the carbon never went through these processes, diamonds would never be formed. Can you see the correlation? God allows us to be exposed to intense circumstances so that we too may become diamonds.

Diamonds are sparkling gems that are many faceted. Diamonds are precious; diamonds are strong. God always has greater plans for our lives that we are often unable to see in the midst of struggling and suffering. But as we press through these processes we emerge as diamonds.

Part 3: The Pressing

The Pressing: Power

One very important lesson I learned as I was pressing through the process was that God Almighty was able to provide me with all of the power I needed to keep on going. Second Corinthians 12:9-10 puts it like this: "My grace (My favor and loving-kindness and mercy) is enough for you [sufficient against any danger and enables you to bear the trouble manfully]; for *My strength and power are made perfect (fulfilled and completed) and show themselves most effective in your weakness...*for when I am weak [in human strength], then I am [truly] strong (able, powerful in divine strength)" (AMPC, emphasis added).

I could not make it through a trial of this magnitude in my own limited, human strength. I had to learn to rely upon God's power which was only available as I acknowledged my weakness and asked Him for His help. Humility includes the realization of who God is and that we need Him.

The Pressing: Protection and Provision

God is always true to His Word. He was always faithful to protect me and my children as well as to provide our needs. A perfect example to illustrate both of these concepts was our house. We lived in a very nice house in an excellent neighborhood, and this house was purchased when we were a two-income household. So when I went from dual income to zero income, I was certain I would have to sell our house and move to a less safe neighborhood just to survive.

However, God had other plans for us. I made several attempts to sell the house, even to the point that my real estate agent said to me, "Carolyn, we have done everything we can do to sell this house short of have a plane fly over with a banner! It is not God's plan for you to move." And there it was! God supplied the finances for the monthly payment and property taxes.

I never missed a payment or made a late payment. Years later, after all of the children were grown, I was able to sell the house and move to another state. Isn't God good? God truly does supply all of our needs and He knows how to bring financial miracles, of which I had many!

The Pressing: Problems and Pitfalls

Now, let me say this. While we are pressing through the process to get to the other side of victory, there are going to be problems and pitfalls. Stuff is going to happen. The car breaks down; the washing machine needs repairs; there is not enough money to get to the end of the month; children are going to have complications, and on and on!

But, God. Yes, but God! We do not stop pressing just because life is full of tribulation. Instead, we keep on advancing in the face of adversity and remember that the problem solver is right there with us, working out every last detail for our good!

Part 4: Conclusion

IN THE MIDST of life's greatest trials, as we continue to press through the process, Jesus, who is the Prince of Peace, is with us. He is using all of these things to work together for our good while at the same time He is perfecting and purifying us. It is possible to be in pain and have peace at the same time; pain and peace can dwell together. The key is to be patient and persistent while allowing God to do a great work in your life.

In spite of the magnitude of the trial, and in spite of all of the microtrials that flooded my life, I kept on praising, praying, and pursuing God. Abiding in His presence was crucial. And when it was all said and done, God had revealed His perfect plan in the process.

It is my prayer that you too will find your strength in Jesus. If you know Him as your Lord and Savior, know that He is in you, with you, and for you. He will walk with you every step of the way. He truly does have all of the power you need to succeed. You won't make it through perfectly, but you *will* make it through. We have to go through to get through, and there are awesome and wonderful blessings on the way.

I encourage you to press on, precious one, and you too can be a Soul Survivor!

Thirty-One Days of Power

TAKE A FEW minutes each day to read the Scripture and corresponding meditation. Then reflect upon what the Holy Spirit is saying to you, and God will restore your soul. If you take the time to journal your thoughts, you will have a written record of what God speaks to you.

DAY 1

"I can do all things through Christ who strengthens me" (Philippians 4:13).

Today I can do anything and everything that I need to do because God will give me the strength.

Reflect:

DAY 2

*"I sought the Lord, and He heard me,
and delivered me from all my fears"*
(Psalm 34:4-5).

God hears me when I call to Him. He sets me free from all of my fears so I can move forward and take the next step.

Reflect:

_____

_____

_____

_____

_____

_____

_____

_____

_____

_____

DAY 3

"The Lord is near to those who have a broken heart and saves such as have a contrite spirit. Many are the afflictions of the righteous, But the Lord delivers him out of them all"
(Psalm 34:18-19).

Even when I don't feel like God is near me, His Word assures me that He is.

Reflect:

_____
_____
_____
_____
_____
_____
_____
_____
_____

DAY 4

"And we know that all things work together for good to those who love God, to those who are the called according to His purpose"
(Romans 8:28).

It's difficult during painful times to understand God's purpose. But God does not waste our pain. Although things don't feel good, they are working together for our good. God loves me even during dark days.

Reflect:

_____

_____

_____

_____

_____

_____

_____

_____

DAY 5

"Fear not, for I have redeemed you; I have called you by your name; You are Mine. When you pass through the waters, I will be with you; and through the rivers they shall not overflow you" (Isaiah 43:1-2).

I can choose to be unafraid! God is with me, and He has promised that my troubles will not overtake me. God knows my name and my confidence is in Him.

Reflect:

_____

_____

_____

_____

_____

_____

_____

_____

DAY 6

"The LORD is my shepherd; I shall not want.
He makes me to lie down in green pastures;
He leads me beside the still waters.
He restores my soul" (Psalm 23:1-3).

God is ordering my steps, and He protects me as a good shepherd protects His sheep. He gives me rest and rebuilds my mind, will, and emotions. I can trust Him.

Reflect:

_____

_____

_____

_____

_____

_____

_____

_____

DAY 7

"I, even I, am He who comforts you"
(Isaiah 51:12).

It's so reassuring to know that God comforts us. And of course, He also sent the Holy Spirit to comfort us in our grief and pain. I can choose to be comforted by His presence when I am hurting.

Reflect:

_____
_____
_____
_____
_____
_____
_____
_____
_____
_____
_____

DAY 8

"And He said to me, 'My grace is sufficient for you, for My strength is made perfect in weakness' "
(2 Corinthians 12:9).

God's supernatural enablement is all that is needed each day to overcome any obstacles we may face. It is because of His grace that I am able to make decisions from a place of strength instead of from a place of weakness.

Reflect:

_____
_____
_____
_____
_____
_____
_____
_____
_____

DAY 9

"What then shall we say to these things?
If God is for us, who can be against us?"
(Romans 8:31).

God is for me; He is with me; He lives in me! Just the knowledge that God is on my side empowers me to move forward. There's nothing I can't do!

Reflect:

_____
_____
_____
_____
_____
_____
_____
_____
_____
_____

DAY 10

"The Lord will perfect that which concerns me"
(Psalm 138:8).

It's reassuring to know that God is taking care of the details. My concerns, my needs, and my desires are important to Him!

Reflect:

_____
_____
_____
_____
_____
_____
_____
_____
_____
_____
_____

DAY 11

"So shall My word be that goes forth from My mouth; It shall not return to Me void, but it shall accomplish what I please, and it shall prosper in the thing for which I sent it" (Isaiah 55:11).

God's Word is powerful, and when we declare what He says over our situation we are destined to be victorious. His promises are not void (empty)!

Reflect:

_____

_____

_____

_____

_____

_____

_____

_____

_____

_____

DAY 12

"And my God shall supply all your need according to His riches in glory by Christ Jesus" (Philippians 4:19).

What a relief to know that everything I *need* (not necessarily want) will be provided by God who has infinite riches! All I need to do is to make my requests known to Him and then eagerly anticipate His supply!

Reflect:

_____
_____
_____
_____
_____
_____
_____
_____
_____

DAY 13

"casting all your care upon Him, for He cares for you" (1 Peter 5:7).

To cast means to throw, hurl, or fling. It's so reassuring to know that I can fling my worries upon Jesus because He cares about me. Yes, He is concerned about all things, great and small, that concern us.

Reflect:

_____
_____
_____
_____
_____
_____
_____
_____
_____
_____

DAY 14

"Is there anything too hard for the LORD?"
(Genesis 18:14).

Whatever it is that you are facing today is not a challenge for God. His power is unlimited, and His promises are true. He will move on your behalf.

Reflect:

DAY 15

*"What is man that You are mindful of him,
And the son of man that You visit him?"*
(Psalm 8:4).

You are on the heart and mind of God. You are precious to Him and He wants to spend time with you. He will visit you, even in the night seasons. He is waiting to hear from you.

Reflect:

_____
_____
_____
_____
_____
_____
_____
_____
_____
_____

DAY 16

"For I know the thoughts I think towards you, says the LORD, thoughts of peace and not of evil, to give you a future and a hope" (Jeremiah 29:11).

God has a marvelous plan for your life. He thinks very highly of you, and it is His delight to reveal His future for you. Let Him fill your heart with the hope of His promises.

Reflect:

_____

_____

_____

_____

_____

_____

_____

_____

_____

DAY 17

"being confident of this very thing, that He who has begun a good work in you will complete it until the day of Jesus Christ" (Philippians 1:6).

God knows what He is doing! You are not God's worst case, and He will finish the good work He has started in you. He is a finisher, and His work is always done to perfection. Stay the course!

Reflect:

_____

_____

_____

_____

_____

_____

_____

_____

_____

DAY 18

"Be anxious for nothing, but in everything by prayer and supplication, with thanksgiving, let your requests be known to God; and the peace of God, which surpasses all understanding, will guard your hearts and minds through Christ Jesus" (Philippians 4:6-7).

Being anxious is human, but it is also a choice. We have the option of presenting our concerns to the God of the universe. We can pray and be thankful that He answers. Choose the peace of God over every anxious thought. God is trustworthy.

Reflect:

_____

_____

_____

_____

_____

_____

DAY 19

"I will instruct you and teach you in the way you should go; I will guide you with My eye" (Psalm 32:8).

When feeling confused, it is so comforting to understand that God Himself will show us exactly what we need to do. He guides us with His eye because He can see everything! There simply is no better instructor than God.

Reflect:

DAY 20

"The earth is full of the goodness of the LORD"
(Psalm 33:5).

We don't have to look too far to see all of the evil and negativity in the world. But when we shift our focus to see all of God's goodness, we find the courage to soar. God is good, and it's important to saturate our lives with all of that goodness.

Reflect:

_____
_____
_____
_____
_____
_____
_____
_____
_____

DAY 21

"I will bless the Lord at all times; His praise shall continually be in my mouth" (Psalm 34:1).

When we bless the Lord and praise Him in the middle of our adverse circumstances, we literally shift the atmosphere and create space for the miraculous! Let us bless Him at all times!

Reflect:

DAY 22

*"I called on the Lord in distress;
The Lord answered me and set me in a broad
place. The Lord is on my side; I will not fear"*
(Psalm 118:5-6).

When we call out to God, He answers! He may not give the exact answer that we expected, but He is all wise and knows the perfect way to answer our prayers. He always wants what is best for us.

Reflect:

_____

_____

_____

_____

_____

_____

_____

_____

DAY 23

*"My help comes from the LORD,
who made heaven and earth"* (Psalm 121:2).

Stop and think. The God who created all of heaven and earth is the One who helps us. The same God who created all of this vastness is the One who assists us. Wow!

Reflect:

DAY 24

*"He gives power to the weak, and to those who have no might He increases strength.... But those who wait on the L*ORD *shall renew their strength; They shall mount up with wings like eagles; they shall run and not be weary. They shall walk and not faint"* (Isaiah 40:29, 31).

If you cannot face one more minute of one more day, find your place in Him. Get on your knees in prayer and ask Him to give you His power and strength. Wait in His presence, and then move forward.

Reflect:

_____

_____

_____

_____

_____

_____

DAY 25

"For with God nothing will be impossible"
(Luke 1:37).

Whatever it is that we need God to do in accordance with His Word, He will do. God is a God of unlimited possibilities. Let's not limit Him with our limited thinking. Won't He do it? Yes, He will!

Reflect:

_____
_____
_____
_____
_____
_____
_____
_____
_____
_____

DAY 26

"Death and life are in the power of the tongue"
(Proverbs 18:21).

Our words are containers of power. It's so important to speak the Word of God over and into our circumstances. When I speak the powerful Word of God, mountains move. What Scriptures can you speak over your life right now?

Reflect:

_____

_____

_____

_____

_____

_____

_____

_____

_____

DAY 27

"But He knows the way that I take; When He has tested me, I shall come forth as gold" (Job 23:10).

God sees you, and His hand is upon your life. Don't think for a minute that He doesn't understand. He is merely turning you into gold!

Reflect:

DAY 28

"Do not be afraid. Stand still and see the salvation of the Lord, which He will accomplish for you today. For the Egyptians whom you see today, you shall see again no more forever. The Lord will fight for you, and you shall hold your peace"
(Exodus 14:13-14).

What do you need God to do? He will fight for you, and when He finishes, these Egyptians, these current troubles, will be gone once and for all. Be at peace and watch Him fight.

Reflect:

_____

_____

_____

_____

_____

_____

_____

DAY 29

"Have I not commanded you? Be strong and of good courage; do not be afraid, nor be dismayed, for the LORD your God is with you wherever you go" (Joshua 1:9).

What a great reassurance to know that God is always with us. We can choose to be courageous, and there is no need to be depressed. God's got this.

Reflect:

_____
_____
_____
_____
_____
_____
_____
_____
_____

DAY 30

"Therefore submit to God. Resist the devil and he will flee from you" (James 4:7).

Place yourself under God's authority and put up a good fight. Fight back and stand your ground; watch the devil flee!!

Reflect:

DAY 31

"Rejoice always, pray without ceasing, in everything give thanks; for this is the will of God in Christ Jesus for you" (1 Thessalonians 5:16-18).

God has given you every single thing you need to succeed! Rejoice; pray; give thanks. With Jesus by your side, you are unstoppable. Go forth and conquer!

Reflect:

_____
_____
_____
_____
_____
_____
_____
_____
_____

Made in the USA
Monee, IL
08 September 2023